DATE DUE

THE

a R T

O F

W A R

by

Sun

Tzu

ADAPTED

AND

INTRODUCED

BY

STEFAN

RUDNICKI

DOVE
BOOKS

ISBN: 0–7871–0561–9

Printed in the United States of America

Dove Books
8955 Beverly Boulevard
West Hollywood, CA 90048

Distributed by Penguin USA

Fighting South of the Castle is translated by Arthur Waley

Designed by David Skolkin

First Printing: June 1996

10 9 8 7 6 5 4 3 2 1

OCT 25 1996

iNTRODUCTION

APPROXIMATELY TWENTY-FIVE HUNDRED YEARS AGO, in a time of political turbulence and great military activity, Sun Tzu, a philosopher-general of ancient China, assembled his observations on warfare into thirteen chapters, creating the classic work known as *The Art of War*. This was a long time ago and times have surely changed, yet this book of "the thirteen chapters" has not only survived, it has exerted an extraordinary influence on the modern world, perhaps particularly in the last ten years or so. People of all persuasions, from all walks of life—buyers and sellers, soldiers and brokers, backers and hackers, inlaws and outlaws—all have found inspiration and sound, practical guidance here.

The period with which Sun Tzu is usually linked, roughly the mid-fourth to the mid-fifth century Before the Common Era, was a high point in the evolution of human wisdom and achievement. Among Sun Tzu's near contemporaries were Lao Tsu, Confucius, Zoroaster, and Gautama Buddha; Pythagoras and Pindar; Heraclitus and Herodotus; Aeschylus, Sophocles, and Aesop; the prophets Ezekiel and Jeremiah; and Pericles of Athens.

Religion, philosophy, music, art, science, and literature flourished. So did war and conquest.

There were fortifications and conflagrations, occupations and liberations, coronations and usurpations. Pharaohs, kings, and tyrants rose and fell; empires were lost and won.

For nearly fifty years, the Romans fought the Etruscans, and the Persians fought the Greeks.

In China, feudal states were at almost constant war. Dynasties rose and fell with cruel regularity. In such a time, a fine balance had to be maintained between the traditional, peaceful civic virtues upon which Chinese culture had been built and other, more militaristic principles. Even Confucius (c. 551–478 B.C.E.), who was probably a contemporary of Sun Tzu and who was known for his advocacy of peace, was quoted as saying: "If I fight, I win."

The historian Ssu-ma Ch'ien, a principal biographer of Sun Tzu writing around 100 B.C.E., said:

2

> When the Duke of Chou was minister under Ch'eng Wang, he regulated ceremonies and made music, and venerated the arts of scholarship and learning. Yet when the barbarians of the river Huai revolted, he sallied forth and chastised them. When Confucius held office under the Duke of Lu,

he said: "If peaceful negotiations are in progress, warlike preparations should have been made beforehand."

Ssu-ma Ch'ien also stated that:

Military weapons are the means used by the Sage to punish violence and cruelty, to give peace to troubled times, to remove difficulties and dangers, and to aid those who are in peril. Every animal with blood in its veins and horns on its head will fight when it is attacked. How much more will man, who carries in his breast the faculties of love and hatred, joy and anger! When he is pleased, a feeling of affection springs up within him. When angry, his poisoned sting is brought into play. That is the natural law which governs his being.

Ssu-ma Ch'ien also said of Sun Tzu that he was a native of the Ch'i State. He told this story about *The Art of War* being brought to the attention of Ho Lu, the reigning King of Wu from 514 to 496 B.C.E.

Ho Lu said to Sun Tzu: "I have carefully perused your thirteen chapters. May I submit your theory of managing soldiers to a little test?"

Sun Tzu replied: "You may."

Ho Lu asked: "May the test be applied to women?"

The answer was again in the affirmative, so arrangements were made to bring one hundred eighty ladies out of the Palace. Sun Tzu divided them into two companies, and placed one of the King's favorite concubines at the head of each. He then bade them all take spears in their hands, and addressed them in this manner: "I presume you know the difference between front and back, right hand and left hand?"

The girls replied: "Yes."

Sun Tzu went on: "When I say 'eyes front,' you must look straight ahead. When I say 'left turn,' you must face toward your left hand. When I say 'right turn,' you must face toward your right hand. When I say 'about turn,' you must face right around toward the back."

Again the girls assented.

The words of command having been thus explained, he set up pikes and battle-axes in order to begin the drill. Then, to the sound of drums, he gave the order "right turn."

But the girls only burst out laughing.

Sun Tzu said: "If words of command are not clear and distinct, if orders are not thoroughly understood, then the general is to blame."

So he started drilling them again, and this time gave the order "left turn," whereupon the girls once more burst into fits of laughter.

Sun Tzu said: "If words of command are not clear and distinct, if orders are not thoroughly understood, the general is to blame. But if his orders *are* clear, and the soldiers nevertheless disobey, then it is the fault of their officers."

So saying, he ordered the leaders of the two companies to be beheaded.

Now the King of Wu was watching the scene from the top of a raised pavilion. And when he saw that his favorite concubines were about to be executed, he was greatly alarmed and hurriedly sent down the following message: "We are now quite satisfied as to our general's ability to handle troops. If We are bereft of these two concubines, our meat and drink will lose their savor. It is our wish that they shall not be beheaded."

Sun Tzu replied: "Having once received His Majesty's commission to be general of his forces, there are certain commands of His Majesty which, acting in that capacity, I am unable to accept."

Accordingly, he had the two leaders beheaded, and straightway installed the pair next in order as leaders in their place. When this had been done, the drum was sounded for the drill once more, and this time the girls went through all the motions, turning to the right or to the left, marching ahead or wheeling back, kneeling or standing, with perfect accuracy and precision, not venturing to utter a sound.

Then Sun Tzu sent a messenger to the King saying: "Your soldiers, Sire, are now properly drilled and disciplined, and ready for Your Majesty's inspection. They can be put to any use that their sovereign may desire. Bid them go through fire and water, and they will not disobey."

But the King replied: "Let our general cease drilling and return to camp. As for us, We have no wish to come down and inspect the troops."

Thereupon Sun Tzu said: "The King is only fond of words, and cannot translate them into deeds."

After that, Ho Lu saw that Sun Tzu was one who knew how to handle an army, and appointed him general.

In the West, Sun Tzu defeated the Ch'u State and forced his way into Ying, the capital. To the North, he put fear into the States of Ch'i and Chin, and spread his fame abroad amongst the feudal princes. And Sun Tzu shared in the might of the King.

Although the story is apocryphal, and Sun Tzu's dates (c. 540?–c. 464? B.C.E.), as well as his authorship of *The Art of War*, are in dispute, the events here described echo the tone of the book. The expendability of individual life in the interest of discipline and absolute authority seems unnecessarily cruel, and many modern translators and commentators are quick to suggest that these elements were meant to be tempered by more humane Confucian or Taoist principles. The fact remains, however, that "the thirteen chapters" are about war. This is not a book of general philosophy, but rather a professional manual. It was meant to be available only to a select few, a kind of secret society of generals and kings, and not to the public at large.

The book's influence spread slowly, to Japan during the eighth century C.E., and from there throughout Asia and into Russia, where it formed the basis of military thought for centuries. It was completely unknown in the West until 1772, when J. J. M. Amiot, a Jesuit missionary to Peking, published his interpretation of *The Art of War* in Paris. Amiot's work was well received and widely circulated, and was published again, in an anthology, in 1782. Legend has it that Napoleon read Sun Tzu, and this may have been the edition. The first English translation, by Captain E. F. Calthrop, R. F. A., did not appear until 1905, and the Lionel Giles translation, from which this version is mostly derived, appeared five years later, in 1910.

For the most part, the commentaries that follow each chapter of Sun Tzu's text in this edition are from a variety of Chinese sources. Several of those cited are considered Sun Tzu's formal commentators. Among the most prominent are the third-century general and military genius Ts'ao Kung; the eighth-century tactician Li Ch'uan; Tu Yu, whose commentaries were culled from his monumental encyclopedic treatise on the Chinese Constitution; and the poets Tu Mu and Mei Yao-ch'en. Their commentaries are augmented by quotes from other Chinese writers and a handful of more modern western personalities including

6

the seventeenth-century French military leader Marshal Turenne and American generals Stonewall Jackson and Colin Powell.

It is popular today to think of *The Art of War* as a practical guidebook for any number of activities that require strategy, from sports and normal business affairs to affairs of the heart. And it *can* be just that, provided that you are willing to see the world in which you live and work as a network of actual and potential combat zones, where the stakes are high, and struggle is the primary mode of being; where no one is to be trusted, and survival depends on unconditional victory. War, then, becomes not merely a metaphor for the conflicts of everyday life, but a state of mind.

Like the oriental martial arts, *The Art of War* emphasizes adaptability and flow, grounding the work firmly in those elements of the Chinese tradition of subtle universal order known to us through the *I Ching (Book of Changes)* and texts like Lao Tsu's *Tao Te Ching*. The very first constant factor discussed in chapter one is the Tao. This is most often translated as Moral Influence or the Moral Law, as the Right Way, or simply, the Way. It is the cosmic cycle of energy rotation and transformation, the flow of all things natural; it is the dynamic that informs the path of least resistance. I have called it the Force, as much for its appropriateness in a military context as for its popular sense, thanks to George Lucas, of a natural, universal energy with which one seeks alignment.

7

The first move is always the opponent's, telling us everything we need to know about his strengths and weaknesses. For our part, we must be sensitive to all the conditions and circumstances that apply, including terrain, climate, cycles of season and time, personality, and politics.

At the same time, we must give away as little as possible about ourselves. All action needs therefore to be built upon the shifting sands of deceit and deliberate obfuscation, our motives and intentions hidden even from our own side. In this, Sun Tzu laid the groundwork for all future espionage systems.

Sun Tzu places great emphasis on the importance of detail, and illustrations abound in statistical terms that seem of little use to us today. After all, the costs of waging war have certainly changed. Chariots, armor, cooking pots, and other ancient implements are no longer the measures they once were. Cost and gain, however, are still key issues, and these details provide us with a keen sense of proportion, always of vital importance to the Chinese.

Perhaps most important to remember are one commentator's suggestion that warlike precepts are not to be applied in peacetime and Sun Tzu's own insistence that the best way of waging war is not to fight at all. This second is not a pacifist statement, but simply a truth about the costs of war. It is then the reader's or listener's moral prerogative to decide whether circumstances warrant engaging in war—whether there is indeed an enemy, whether the cost of the battle will be worth the prize, and whether we are willing to risk *all* to achieve victory.

To hear the answer, we must listen, both within ourselves and without, to the thousands of signals the natural world provides. We must listen to the Tao, we must attend the Force.

8

Lao
Tsu
said:

Before Heaven and Earth,
Undefined, yet complete,
Formless,
Standing alone, unchanging,
Reaching everywhere.
It is the mother of all things.

I do not know its name.

I call it the Force.
Upon further reflection, I name it the Great.

Because it is great, it is in constant flow.
Passing on, it becomes distant.
Then it returns.

Therefore, the Force is great.
Heaven is great.
Earth is great.
The King is also great.
There are four great powers in the universe.
The King is one of them.

Man takes his law from the Earth.
Earth takes its law from Heaven.
Heaven takes its law from the Force.
The law of the Force is to be what it is.

9

*An introduction
to the five
constant factors,
the seven
considerations,
deception, and
calculation.*

*L*AYING PLANS

*Sun
Tzu
said:*

THE ART OF WAR IS OF VITAL IMPORTANCE TO THE STATE. It is a matter of life and death, a road either to safety or to ruin. Hence it is a subject for study that can on no account be neglected.

The art of war is governed by five constant factors, all of which need to be considered. These are: The Force, Heaven, Earth, the Commander, and Discipline.

• The Force causes the people to be in complete accord with their ruler, so that they will follow him regardless of their lives, undismayed by any danger.

• Heaven signifies night and day, cold and heat, seasons, and cycles of the moon.

• Earth comprises distances, great and small; danger and security; open ground and narrow passes; the chances of life and death.

• The Commander stands for the virtues of wisdom, sincerity, benevolence, courage, and strictness.

• Discipline is to be understood as the marshaling of the army in its proper subdivisions, the gradations of rank among the officers, the maintenance of roads by which supplies may reach the army, and the control of military expenditure.

These five factors should be familiar to every general. He who knows them will be victorious. He who knows them not will fail.

Therefore, when seeking to determine the military conditions, make your decisions on the basis of comparison, utilizing the seven considerations, in this wise:

1. Which of the two sovereigns is imbued with the Force?

2. Which of the two generals has the most ability?

3. With whom lie the advantages derived from Heaven and Earth?

4. On which side is discipline most rigorously enforced?

5. Which army is the stronger?

6. On which side are officers and men more highly trained?

7. In which army is there the greater constancy, both in reward and in punishment?

By means of these seven considerations I can forecast victory or defeat.

The general who hearkens to my counsel and acts upon it will conquer—let such a one be retained in command! The general who hearkens not to my counsel nor acts upon it will suffer defeat—let such a one be dismissed!

While heeding the profit of my counsel, avail yourself also of any helpful circumstances over and beyond the ordinary rules. Plans should be modified to reflect favorable or unfavorable circumstances.

All warfare is based on deception. Hence, when able to attack, we must seem unable. When using our forces, we must seem inactive. When we are near, we must make the enemy believe we are far away. When far away, we must make him believe we are near. Hold out baits to entice the enemy. Feign disorder, and crush him. If he is secure at all points, be prepared for him. If he is superior in strength, evade him. If your opponent is quick to anger, seek to irritate him. Pretend to be weak, that he may grow arrogant. If he is taking his ease, give him no rest. If his forces are united, separate them. Attack him where he is unprepared; appear where you are not expected.

These military devices lead to victory, and they must not be divulged beforehand.

The general who wins a battle makes many calculations in his temple before the battle is fought. The general who loses a battle makes only a few calculations beforehand. Thus do many calculations lead to victory, and few calculations to defeat; how much more no calculation at all! It is by attention to this point that I can foresee who is likely to win or lose.

COMMENTARIES

Ts'ao Ts'ao
said this
about Discipline:

When you lay down a law, see that it is not disobeyed. If it is disobeyed, the offender must be put to death.

Tu Mu
told this
story:

There was a general, Ts'ao Ts'ao, who was such a strict disciplinarian that once, in accordance with his own severe regulations against injury to standing crops, he condemned himself to death for having allowed his horse to shy into a field of corn. However, in lieu of losing his head, he was persuaded to satisfy his sense of justice by cutting off his hair.

Chang Yu said
of planning:

While the main laws of strategy can be stated clearly enough for the benefit of all, you must be guided by the actions of the enemy in attempting to secure a favorable position in actual warfare.

13

Sir W. Fraser
tells this story:

On the eve of the battle of Waterloo, Lord Uxbridge, commanding the cavalry, went to the Duke of Wellington in order to learn what his plans and calculations were for the morrow, because, as he explained, he might suddenly find himself Commander-in-chief and would be unable to frame new plans in a critical moment. The Duke listened quietly and then said, "Who will attack the first tomorrow—I or Bonaparte?" "Bonaparte," replied Lord Uxbridge. "Well," continued the Duke, "Bonaparte has not given me any idea of his projects; and as my plans will depend upon his, how can you expect me to tell you what mine are?"

chapter

two

The economics of war, and the importance of speed.

W AGING WAR

Sun Tzu said:

IN THE OPERATIONS OF WAR, where there are in the field a thousand swift chariots, a thousand heavy chariots, and a hundred thousand mail-clad soldiers, with provisions enough to carry them a thousand *li*, the expenditure at home and at the front, including entertainment of guests, small items such as glue and paint, and sums spent on chariots and armor, will reach the total of a thousand ounces of silver per day. Such is the cost of raising an army of a hundred thousand men.

When you engage in actual fighting, if victory is long in coming, the men's weapons will grow dull and their

15

ardor will dampen. If you lay siege to a town, you will exhaust your strength. If the campaign is protracted, the resources of the state will not be equal to the strain. When your weapons are dulled, your ardor dampened, your strength exhausted, and your treasure spent, other chieftains will spring up to take advantage of your extremity. Then no man, however wise, will be able to avert the inevitable consequences.

Thus, though we have heard of stupid haste in war, cleverness has never been seen associated with long delays. There is no instance of a country having benefited from prolonged warfare. Only one who knows the disastrous effects of a long war can realize the supreme importance of speed in bringing it to a close.

The skillful leader does not raise a second levy; neither are his supply wagons loaded more than twice. Once war is declared, he will not waste precious time in waiting for reinforcements, nor will he turn his army back for fresh supplies. He will cross the enemy's frontier with no delay.

Bring war material with you from home, but forage on the enemy. In this way the army will have food enough for its needs. Poverty of the state exchequer causes an army to be maintained by contributions from a distance. Contributing to maintain an army at a distance causes the people to be impoverished.

On the other hand, the proximity of an army causes prices to go up, and high prices cause the people's substance to be drained away. When their substance is drained away, they will be afflicted by heavy exactions. With this loss of substance and exhaustion of strength, the homes of the people will be stripped bare, and three-tenths of their incomes will be dissipated, while government expenses for broken chariots, worn-out horses, breastplates and helmets, bows and arrows, spears and shields, protective mantlets, draught oxen and heavy wagons, will amount to four-tenths of its total revenue.

Hence a wise general makes a point of foraging on the enemy. One cartload of the enemy's provisions is equivalent to twenty of one's own, and likewise a single pound of his provisions is equivalent to twenty from one's own store.

Now, in order to kill the enemy, our men must be roused to anger. That there may be advantage from defeating the enemy, they must have their rewards.

Therefore in chariot fighting, when ten or more chariots have been taken, those should be rewarded who took the first. Our own flags should be substituted for those of the enemy, and the chariots mingled and used in conjunction with ours. The captured soldiers should be kindly treated and kept. This is called using the conquered foe to augment one's own strength.

In war, then, let your objective be victory, not lengthy campaigns. Thus it may be known that the leader of armies is the arbiter of the people's fate, the man on whom it depends whether the nation shall be in peace or in peril.

COMMENTARIES

Of rewards,
Tu Mu said:

17

Rewards are necessary in order to make the soldiers see the advantage of beating the enemy. Thus, when you capture spoils from the enemy, they must be used as rewards, so that all your men may have a keen desire to fight, each on his own account.

*General Colin
Powell has said:*

Nobody in his right mind who has seen war, who has seen death and war, can like war or want war.

*Colin Powell
also said:*

There should be no use of force unless success is all but guaranteed. Force should be used decisively and its application should preferably be short. As soon as the aims are achieved, American forces should be quickly extracted, lest the military fall into a quagmire.

*Lionel Giles
noted:*

As for units of measurement, there are 2.78 *li* to the mile. And as for numbers of troops, in early Chinese warfare, as with the Homeric Greeks, the war chariot formed the nucleus around which were grouped certain numbers of foot soldiers; in this case, seventy-five to each swift chariot, and twenty-five to each heavy chariot.

Basic strategies,

not fighting

at all, the

five essentials

for victory.

*a*TTACK BY STRATAGEM

Sun
Tzu
said:

IN THE PRACTICAL ART OF WAR, the best thing of all is to take the enemy's country whole and intact. To shatter and destroy it is not so good. So, too, it is better to capture an army than to destroy it. It is better to capture a whole regiment, an entire detachment, or a full company, than to destroy them.

Hence, to fight and conquer in all your battles is not supreme excellence. Supreme excellence consists in breaking the enemy's resistance without fighting.

Thus the highest form of leadership is to thwart the enemy's plans. The next best is to prevent the junction of the enemy's forces. The next in order is to attack the enemy's army in the field. And the worst policy of all is to besiege walled cities. The rule is, not to besiege walled cities if it can possibly be avoided, for the preparation of defensive screens, movable shelters, and various implements of war will take up three whole months; and the piling up of mounds over against the walls will take three months more. The general, unable to control his irritation, will launch his men to the assault like swarming ants, with the result that one-third of his men are slain, while the town still remains untaken. Such are the disastrous effects of a siege.

Therefore the skillful leader subdues the enemy's troops without any fighting. He captures their cities without laying siege to them. He overthrows their kingdom without lengthy operations in the field. With his forces intact he disputes the mastery of the empire, and without losing a man, his triumph is complete. The weapon, not being blunted by use, remains sharp and perfect.

This is the method of attacking by stratagem.

It is the rule in war:

- If our forces are ten to the enemy's one, surround him.

- If our forces are five to his one, attack him.

- If equally matched, we can offer battle.

- If slightly inferior in numbers, we can avoid the enemy.

- If quite unequal to the enemy in every way, we can flee from him.

Though an obstinate fight may be made by a small force, in the end it must be captured by the larger force.

The general is the bulwark of the state. If the bulwark is strong at all points, the state will be strong. If the bulwark is defective, the state will be weak.

There are three ways in which a sovereign can bring misfortune upon his general and his army:

1. By commanding the army to advance or to retreat, being ignorant of the fact that it cannot obey. This is called hobbling the army.

2. By attempting to govern an army in the same way as he administers a kingdom, being ignorant of the conditions that obtain in an army. This causes restlessness in the soldiers' minds.

3. By employing the officers of his army without discrimination, through ignorance of the military principle of adaptation to circumstances, This shakes the confidence of the soldiers, and when the army is restless and distrustful, trouble is sure to come from the other feudal princes. This is simply bringing anarchy into the army, and flinging victory away.

Thus we may know that there are five essentials for victory:

1. He will win who knows when to fight and when not to fight.

2. He will win who knows how to handle both superior and inferior forces.

3. He will win whose army is animated by the same spirit throughout all its ranks.

4. He will win who, prepared himself, waits to take the enemy unprepared.

5. He will win who has military capacity and is not interfered with by the sovereign.

Victory lies in the knowledge of these five points. Hence the saying: If you know the enemy and know yourself, you need not fear the result of a hundred battles. If you know yourself but not the enemy, for every victory gained you will suffer a defeat. If you know neither the enemy nor yourself, you will succumb in every battle.

COMMENTARIES

Of advantage
in numbers,
Chang Yu said:

If our forces are twice as numerous, divide our army into two, one to meet the enemy in front, and one to fall upon his rear. If he replies to the frontal attack, he may be crushed from behind. If to the rearward attack, he may be crushed in front.

He further
reminds us that:

A small difference in numbers is often more than counterbalanced by superior energy and discipline. By applying the art of war, it is possible with a lesser force to defeat a greater, and vice versa. The secret lies in an eye for locality, and in not letting the right moment slip.

On the difference
between governing
the state and the
army, he said:

Humanity and justice are the principles on which to govern the state, but not an army. Opportunism and flexibility, on the other hand, are military rather than civic virtues.

Referring to the
principle of adaptability
in employing officers,
Tu Mu quoted:

The skillful employer of men will employ the wise man, the brave man, the covetous man, and the stupid man. For the wise man delights in establishing his merit, the brave man likes to show his courage in action, the covetous man is quick at seizing advantages, and the stupid man has no fear of death.

*t*ACTICS

Sun
Tzu
said:

THE GOOD FIGHTERS OF OLD FIRST put themselves beyond the possibility of defeat, and then waited for an opportunity of defeating the enemy.

To secure ourselves against defeat lies in our own hands, but the opportunity of defeating the enemy is provided by the enemy himself. Thus the good fighter is able to secure himself against defeat, but cannot make certain of defeating the enemy.

Hence the saying: One may *know* how to conquer without being able to *do* it.

Security against defeat implies defensive tactics. Ability to defeat the enemy means taking the offensive. Standing on the defensive indicates insufficient strength. Attacking indicates a superabundance of strength.

The general who is skilled in defense hides in the most secret recesses of the earth. He who is skilled in attack flashes forth from the topmost heights of heaven like a thunderbolt, against which there is not time to prepare. Thus, on the one hand, we have ability to protect ourselves; on the other, a victory that is complete.

To see victory only when it is within sight of the common herd is not the height of excellence. Nor is it the height of excellence if you fight and conquer and the whole empire says, "Well done!" To lift a hair is no sign of great strength. To see the sun and the moon is no sign of sharp sight. To hear the noise of thunder is no sign of a quick ear.

What the ancients called a clever fighter is one who not only wins, but excels in winning with ease. His victories bring him neither reputation for wisdom nor credit for courage.

He wins his battle by making no mistakes. Making no mistakes is what establishes the certainty of victory, for it means conquering an enemy that is already defeated.

Hence the skillful fighter puts himself into a position that makes defeat impossible and does not miss the moment for defeating the enemy.

Thus it is that in war the victorious strategist only seeks battle after the victory has been won, whereas he who is destined to defeat, fights, and afterward looks for victory.

The consummate leader cultivates the Force and strictly adheres to method and discipline. Thus it is in his power to control success.

In respect of military method, we have:

1. Measurement
2. Estimation of quantity
3. Calculation
4. Balancing of chances
5. Victory

Measurement owes its existence to Earth, Estimation of quantity to Measurement, Calculation to Estimation of quantity, Balancing of chances to Calculation, and Victory to Balancing of chances.

A victorious army opposed to a routed one is as a pound's weight placed in the scale against a single grain. The onrush of a conquering force is like the bursting of pent-up waters into a chasm a thousand fathoms deep.

This is all there is to be said about tactics.

COMMENTARIES

Tu Mu
said:

True excellence is to plan secretly, to move surreptitiously, to foil the enemy's intentions and thwart his schemes, so that at last the day may be won without shedding a drop of blood. Inasmuch as such victories are gained over circumstances that have not yet come to light, the world at large knows nothing of them, and the clever fighter wins no reputation for wisdom. Inasmuch as the hostile state submits before there has been any bloodshed, he receives no credit for courage.

*Chang Yu
added:*

One who seeks to conquer by sheer strength, clever though he may be at winning pitched battles, is also liable on occasion to be vanquished, whereas he who can look into the future and discern conditions that are not yet manifest will never make a blunder and therefore invariably win.

*And Ts'ao
Kung remarked:*

The thing is to see the plant before it has germinated, to foresee the event before the action has begun.

*Li Ch'uan
told this story:*

Han Hsin, when about to attack a vastly superior army, said to his officers, "Gentlemen, we are going to annihilate the enemy, and shall meet again at dinner." The officers hardly took his words seriously, and gave a very dubious assent. But Han Hsin had already worked out in his mind the details of a clever stratagem, whereby, as he foresaw it, he was able to capture the city and inflict a crushing defeat on his adversary.

*Referring to Measurement
and its corollaries,
Tu Mu concluded:*

27

The question of relative strength having been settled, we can bring the varied resources of cunning into play.

Direct and
indirect maneuvers,
the power of
decision,
combined energy.

eNERGY AND POWER

Sun
Tzu
said:

THE CONTROL OF A LARGE FORCE is the same in principle as the control of a few men. It is merely a question of dividing up their numbers. Fighting with a large army under your command is in no way different from fighting with a small one. It is merely a question of instituting signs and signals.

To ensure that your whole host may withstand the brunt of the enemy's attack and remain unshaken, use both direct and indirect maneuvers.

That the impact of your army may be like a grindstone dashed against an egg—this is effected by the science of weak points and strong, the hollow and the solid.

In all fighting, the direct method may be used for joining battle, but indirect methods will be needed in order to secure victory.

Indirect tactics, efficiently applied, are as inexhaustible as Heaven and Earth, unending as the flow of rivers and streams. Like the sun and moon, they end but to begin anew. Like the four seasons, they pass away but to return once more.

There are not more than five musical notes, yet the combinations of these five give rise to more melodies than can ever be heard. There are not more than five primary colors, yet in combination they produce more hues than can ever be seen. There are not more than five cardinal tastes—sour, acrid, salt, sweet, bitter—yet combinations of them yield more flavors than can ever be tasted.

In battle, there are not more than two methods of attack—the direct and the indirect. Yet these two in combination give rise to an endless series of maneuvers. The direct and the indirect lead on to each other in turn. It is like moving in a circle—you never come to an end. Who can exhaust the possibilities of their combination?

The onset of troops is like the rush of a torrent that will even roll stones along in its course. The power of decision is like the well-timed swoop of a falcon that enables it to strike and destroy its victim. Therefore the good fighter will be terrible in his onset, and prompt in his decision.

Energy may be likened to the bending of a crossbow. Decision may be likened to the releasing of the trigger.

Amid the turmoil and tumult of battle, there may be seeming disorder and yet no real disorder at all. Amid confusion and chaos, your array may be without head or tail, yet it will be proof against defeat. Simulated disorder postulates perfect discipline. Simulated fear postulates courage. Simulated weakness postulates strength. Hiding order beneath the cloak of disorder is simply a question of subdivision. Concealing courage under a show of timidity presupposes a fund of latent energy. Masking strength with weakness is to be effected by tactical dispositions.

Thus one who is skillful at keeping the enemy on the move maintains deceitful appearances, according to which the enemy will act. He sacrifices something that the enemy may snatch at it. By holding out baits, he keeps him on the march. Then with a body of picked men he lies in wait for him.

The clever combatant looks to the effect of combined energy, and does not require too much from individuals. Hence his ability to pick out the right men and to utilize combined energy.

When he utilizes combined energy, his fighting men become, as it were, like rolling logs or stones. For it is the nature of a log or stone to remain motionless on level ground, and to move when on a slope. It is also in the nature of a log or a stone, if square, to come to a standstill, but if round-shaped, to go rolling down. Thus the energy developed by good fighting men is as the momentum of a round stone rolled down a mountain thousands of feet in height.

So much for the subject of energy.

30

COMMENTARIES

Tu Mu reminds us of Han Hsin's famous reply to the first Han Emperor, who once said to him: "How large an army do you think I could lead?" "Not more than one hundred thousand men, your Majesty." "And you?" asked the Emperor. "Oh!" he answered, "the more the better."

On direct and indirect, it was said:

In war, to march straight ahead is *cheng*. Turning movements, on the other hand, are *ch'i*.

*Emperor
T'ai Tsung said:*

A *ch'i* (indirect) maneuver may be *cheng* (direct), if we make the enemy look upon it as *cheng*. Then our real attack will be *ch'i*, and vice versa. The whole secret lies in confusing the enemy, so that he cannot fathom our real intent.

*Lionel Giles
observes:*

There is emphasis on proper timing here, and restraint, like that which keeps the falcon from swooping on its quarry until the right moment. There is also the matter of judging when the right moment has arrived.

*Wang Hsi referred to the
falcon's mode of attack,
"short and sharp," and said:*

This is how the psychological moment should be seized in war.

31

*Tu Mu
said:*

If you wish to feign confusion in order to lure the enemy on, you must first have perfect discipline. If you wish to display timidity in order to entrap the enemy, you must first have extreme courage. If you wish to parade your weakness in order to make the enemy over-confident, you must have exceeding strength.

> *Chang Yu related*
> *this anecdote of*
> *Emperor Kao Tsu:*

Wishing to crush the Hsiung-nu, he sent out spies to report on their condition. But the Hsiung-nu, forewarned, carefully concealed all their able-bodied men and well-fed horses, and only allowed infirm soldiers and emaciated cattle to be seen. The result was that the spies one and all recommended to the Emperor to deliver his attack. Lou Ching alone opposed them, saying: "When two countries go to war, they are naturally inclined to make an ostentatious display of their strength. Yet our spies have seen nothing but old age and infirmity. This is surely some ruse on the part of the enemy, and it would be unwise for us to attack." The Emperor, however, disregarding this advice, fell into the trap and found himself surrounded.

> *Tu Mu pointed*
> *out the converse:*

If one's force happens to be superior to the enemy's, weakness may be simulated in order to lure him on; but if inferior, he must be led to believe that we are strong, in order that he may keep off. In fact, all the enemy's movements should be determined by the signs that we choose to give him.

*Tu Mu relates
this anecdote:*

Sun Pin and T'ien Chi, leaders of the Ch'i state, were sent against the general P'ang Chuan of Wei. Sun Pin said: "Our side has a reputation for cowardice, and therefore our adversary despises us. Let us turn this circumstance to our advantage." Accordingly, when the army had crossed the border into Wei territory, he gave orders to show one hundred thousand fires on the first night, fifty thousand on the next, and the night after only twenty thousand. P'ang Chuan pursued them hotly, saying to himself: "I knew these men were cowards. Their numbers have already fallen away by more than half." In his retreat, Sun Pin came to a narrow defile, which he calculated that his pursuers would reach after dark. Here he had a tree stripped of its bark, and inscribed upon it the words: "Under this tree shall P'ang Chuan die." Then, as night began to fall, he placed a strong body of archers in ambush nearby, with orders to shoot the moment they saw a light. Later on, P'ang Chuan arrived at the spot, and, noticing the tree, struck a light in order to read what was written on it. His body was immediately riddled by a volley of arrows, and his whole army thrown into confusion.

*On matters of
combined energy,
Tu Mu stated:*

33

The General first of all considers the power of his army in bulk. Afterward, he takes individual talent into account, and uses each man according to his capabilities. He does not demand perfection from the untalented.

Speed and distance,
secrecy and
concealment,
the infinite variety
of circumstances.

WEAK
POINTS
AND
STRONG

*Sun
Tzu
said:*

WHOEVER IS FIRST IN THE FIELD and awaits the coming of
the enemy will be fresh for the fight. Whoever is second in
the field, and has to hasten to battle, will arrive exhausted.
Therefore the clever combatant imposes his will on the
enemy, but does not allow the enemy's will to be imposed
on him. By holding out advantages to him—enticing him
with a bait—he can cause the enemy to approach of his
own accord; or, by inflicting damage—striking at some
important point which the enemy will have to defend—he
can make it impossible for the enemy to draw near.

If the enemy is taking his ease, he can harass him. If the enemy is well supplied with food, he can starve him out. If the enemy is quietly encamped, he can force him to move.

Appear at points that the enemy must hasten to defend. March swiftly to places where you are not expected.

An army may march great distances without distress if it marches through country where the enemy is not. You can be sure of succeeding in your attacks if you only attack places that are undefended. You can ensure the safety of your defense if you only hold positions that cannot be attacked. That general is skillful in attack whose opponent does not know what to defend, and he is skillful in defense whose opponent does not know what to attack.

O divine art of subtlety and secrecy! Through you we learn to be invisible and unheard, and hence we can hold the enemy's fate in our hands.

You may advance and be absolutely irresistible if you make for the enemy's weak points. You may retire and be safe from pursuit if your movements are more rapid than those of the enemy.

If we wish to fight, the enemy can be forced to an engagement even if he is sheltered behind a high rampart and a deep ditch. All we need do is to attack some other place that he will be obliged to relieve.

If we do not wish to fight, even though the battle lines are drawn, we can prevent the enemy from engaging us. All we need do is to throw something odd and unaccountable in his way to distract him.

By discovering the enemy's dispositions and remaining invisible ourselves, we can keep our forces concentrated, while the enemy's must be divided. We can form a single united body, while the enemy must split up into fractions. Hence there will be a whole pitted against separate parts of a whole, which means that we shall be many to the enemy's few. And if we are able thus to attack an inferior force with a superior one, our opponents will be in dire straits.

The spot where we intend to fight must not be made known, for then the enemy will have to prepare against a possible attack at several different points; and his forces being thus distributed in many directions, the numbers we shall have to face at any given point will be proportionately few.

For should the enemy strengthen his front lines, he will weaken his rear. Should he strengthen his rear, he will weaken the front. Should he strengthen his left, he will weaken his right. Should he strengthen his right, he will weaken his left. If he sends reinforcements everywhere, he will everywhere be weak.

Numerical weakness comes from having to prepare against possible attacks. Numerical strength comes from compelling our adversary to make these preparations against us. Knowing the place and the time of the coming battle, we may concentrate from the greatest distances in order to fight. But if neither time nor place be known, then the left wing will be impotent to succor the right, the right equally impotent to succor the left, the front lines unable to relieve the rear, or the rear to support the front. How much more so if the farthest portions of the army are a hundred *li* apart, and even the nearest are separated by several *li*!

Though the soldiers of the enemy exceed our own in number, this shall not win them victory. I say then that victory can be achieved. Though the enemy be stronger in numbers, we may prevent him from fighting.

Scheme so as to discover his plans and the likelihood of their success. Rouse him, and learn the principle of his activity or inactivity. Force him to reveal himself, so as to find out his vulnerable spots. Carefully compare the opposing army with your own, so that you may know where strength is superabundant and where it is deficient.

In making tactical dispositions, the highest pitch you can attain is to conceal them. Conceal your dispositions, and you will be safe from the prying of the subtlest spies, and from the machinations of the wisest brains.

How victory may be produced for them out of the enemy's own tactics—that is what the multitude cannot comprehend.

All men can see the individual tactics whereby I conquer, but none can see the strategy out of which total victory is evolved.

Do not repeat the tactics which have gained you one victory, but let your methods be regulated by the infinite variety of circumstances.

Military tactics are like water; for water in its natural course runs away from high places and hastens downward. So in war, the way of the Force is to avoid what is strong and to strike at what is weak. Water shapes its course according to the nature of the ground over which it flows. The soldier works out his victory in relation to the foe whom he is facing.

Therefore, just as water retains no constant shape, so in warfare there are no constant conditions. He who can modify his tactics in relation to his opponent, and thereby succeed in winning, may be called a heaven-born captain.

The five elements—water, fire, wood, metal, earth— are not always equally predominant. The four seasons make way for each other in turn. There are short days and long. The moon has its periods of waning and waxing.

COMMENTARIES

Chang Yu
said:

He who is skilled in attack flashes forth from the topmost heights of heaven, making it impossible for the enemy to guard against him. This being so, the places that he shall attack are precisely those that the enemy cannot defend. He who is skilled in defense hides in the most secret recesses of the earth, making it impossible for the enemy to estimate his whereabouts. This being so, the places that he shall hold are precisely those that the enemy cannot attack.

If the enemy's dispositions are visible, we can make for him in one body; whereas, our own dispositions being kept secret, the enemy will be obliged to divide his forces in order to guard against attack from every quarter.

38

Tu Mu
said:

If the enemy is the invading party, we can cut his line of communications and occupy the roads by which he will have to return. If we are the invaders, we may direct our attack against the sovereign himself.

He also told
this anecdote
about distracting
the enemy:

Chu-ko Liang, when occupying Yang-p'ing city and about to be attacked by Ssu-ma the First, suddenly dropped his flags, stopped the beating of the drums, and flung open the city gates, showing only a few men engaged in sweeping and sprinkling the ground. This unexpected proceeding had the intended effect, for Ssu-ma the First, suspecting an ambush, actually drew off his army and retreated.

*The art
of handling
large masses
of men.*

M ANEUVERING

*Sun
Tzu
said:*

IN WAR, THE GENERAL receives his commands from the sovereign.

Having collected an army and concentrated his forces, he must blend and harmonize the different elements thereof before pitching his camp.

After that comes tactical maneuvering. The difficulty of tactical maneuvering consists in turning the devious into the direct, and misfortune into gain. Thus, to take a long and circuitous route after enticing the enemy out of the way, and, though starting after him, to contrive to reach the goal before him, shows knowledge of the artifice of *deviation*.

Maneuvering with an army is advantageous. Maneuvering with an undisciplined multitude is most dangerous. If you set a fully equipped army to march in order to snatch an advantage, the chances are that you will be too late. On the other hand, to detach a flying column for the purpose involves the sacrifice of its baggage and stores.

Thus, if you order your men to pack up their equipment and make forced marches without halting day or night, covering double the usual distance at a stretch, and doing a hundred *li* in order to wrest an advantage, the leaders of your three divisions will fall into the hands of the enemy. The stronger men will be in front, the jaded ones will fall behind, and on this plan only one-tenth of your army will reach its destination. If you march fifty *li* in order to outmaneuver the enemy, you will lose the leader of your first division, and only half your force will reach the goal. If you march thirty *li* with the same objective, two-thirds of your army will arrive. We may take it then that an army without its baggage train is lost. Without provisions it is lost. Without bases of supply it is lost.

We cannot enter into alliances until we are acquainted with the designs of our neighbors.

We are not fit to lead an army on the march unless we are familiar with the face of the country—its mountains and forests, its pitfalls and precipices, its marshes and swamps. We shall be unable to turn natural advantages to account unless we make use of local guides.

In war, practice dissimulation and you will succeed.

Move only if there is a real advantage to be gained. Whether to concentrate or to divide your troops must be decided by circumstances. Let your speed be that of the wind, your compactness that of the forest. In raiding and plundering be like fire. In immovability be like a mountain.

Let your plans be dark and impenetrable as night, and when you move, fall like a thunderbolt.

When you plunder a countryside, let the spoil be divided among your men. When you capture new territory, cut it up into allotments for the benefit of the soldiery.

Ponder and deliberate before you make a move. He will conquer who has learned the artifice of deviation.

Such is the art of maneuvering.

The ancient Book of
Army Management says:

On the field of battle, the spoken word does not carry far enough; hence the institution of gongs and drums.

Nor can ordinary objects be seen clearly enough; hence the institution of banners and flags.

Gongs and drums, banners and flags, these are means whereby the ears and eyes of the host may be focused on one particular point. The host thus forming a single united body, it is impossible either for the brave to advance alone, or for the cowardly to retreat alone.

This is the art of handling large masses of men.

In night fighting, then, make much use of signal fires and drums; and in fighting by day, of flags and banners, as a means of influencing the ears and eyes of your army.

42

A whole army may be robbed of its spirit. A commander-in-chief may be robbed of his presence of mind.

Now a soldier's spirit is keenest in the morning. By noonday it has begun to flag. And in the evening, his mind is bent only on returning to camp. A clever general, therefore, avoids an enemy when its spirit is keen, but attacks it when it is sluggish and inclined to return. This is the art of studying moods.

Disciplined and calm, to await the appearance of disorder and hubbub among the enemy—this is the art of retaining self-possession.

To be near the goal while the enemy is still far from it, to wait at ease while the enemy is toiling and struggling, to be well fed while the enemy is famished—this is the art of conserving one's strength.

To refrain from intercepting an enemy whose banners are in perfect order, to refrain from attacking an army drawn up in calm and confident array—this is the art of studying circumstances.

It is a military axiom not to advance uphill against the enemy, nor to oppose him when he comes downhill.

Do not pursue an enemy who simulates flight. Do not attack soldiers whose temper is keen. Do not swallow a bait offered by the enemy.

Do not interfere with an army that is returning home.

When you surround an army, leave an outlet free. Do not press a desperate foe too hard.

Such is the art of warfare.

C O M M E N T A R I E S

Wu Tzu
said:

Without harmony in the State, no military expedition can be undertaken. Without harmony in the army, no battle array can be formed.

Sun Tzu himself
was quoted as saying:

Those who are waging war should get rid of all domestic troubles before proceeding to attack the external foe.

Tu Mu cited the famous march of
Chao She to relieve the town of O-yu,
which was closely besieged by a Ch'in army:

The King of Chao first consulted Lien P'o on the advisability of attempting a relief, but the latter thought the distance too great, and the intervening country too rugged and difficult. His Majesty then turned to Chao She, who fully admitted the hazardous nature of the march, but finally said: "We shall be like two rats fighting in a hole, and the pluckier one will win." So he left the capital with his army, but had only gone a distance of thirty *li* when he stopped and began throwing up entrenchments. For twenty-eight days he continued strengthening his fortifications, and took care that spies should carry the intelligence to the enemy. The Ch'in general was overjoyed to learn of Chao's tardiness. But the spies had no sooner departed than Chao She began a forced march lasting for two days and one night, and arrived on the scene of action with such astonishing rapidity that he was able to occupy a commanding position before the enemy had got wind of his movements.

*Ts'ao Kung
pointed out:*

Don't march a hundred *li* to gain a tactical advantage. Maneuvers of this sort should be confined to short distances.

*Stonewall
Jackson said:*

The hardships of forced marches are often more painful than the dangers of battle.

*Lionel Giles notes the following
regarding General Jackson:*

It was only when he intended a surprise, or when a rapid retreat was imperative, that he sacrificed everything to speed.

Ch'en Hao quoted the saying:

Birds and beasts when brought to bay will use their claws and teeth.

*Chang Yu
said:*

45

If your adversary has burned his boats and destroyed his cooking pots, and is ready to stake all on the issue of a battle, he must not be pushed to extremities.

Ho Shih told a
story about this:

Fu Yen-ch'ing, a general, was surrounded by a vastly superior barbarian army. The country was bare and desert-like, and his little force was soon in dire straits for want of water. The wells they bored ran dry, and the men were reduced to squeezing lumps of mud and sucking out the moisture. Their ranks thinned rapidly, until at last Fu Yen-ch'ing exclaimed: "We are desperate men. Far better to die for our country than to go with fettered hands into captivity!" A strong gale happened to be blowing from the northeast and darkening the air with dense clouds of sandy dust. An officer named Li Shou-cheng saw an opportunity, and said: "They are many and we are few, but in the midst of this sandstorm our numbers will not be discernible. Victory will go to the strenuous fighter, and the wind will be our best ally." Accordingly, Fu Yen-ch'ing made a sudden and wholly unexpected onslaught with his cavalry, routed the barbarians, and succeeded in breaking through to safety.

Advantage and

disadvantage,

the infinite

variation of

tactics, the

five faults.

tHE NINE VARIATIONS

Sun
Tzu
said:

IN WAR, THE GENERAL receives his commands from the sovereign, collects his army, and concentrates his forces.

When in difficult country, do not encamp. In country where high roads intersect, join hands with your allies. Do not linger in dangerously isolated positions. In hemmed-in situations, you must resort to stratagem. In a desperate position, you must fight.

There are :

• roads which must not be followed;

- armies which must not be attacked;

- towns which must not be besieged;

- positions which must not be contested;

- commands of the sovereign which must not be obeyed.

The general who thoroughly understands the advantages that accompany variation of tactics knows how to handle his troops. The general who does not understand these may be well acquainted with the configuration of the country, yet he will not be able to turn his knowledge to practical account.

In the wise leader's plans, considerations of advantage and of disadvantage will be blended together. If our expectation of advantage be tempered in this way, we may succeed in accomplishing the essential part of our schemes. If, on the other hand, in the midst of difficulties we are always ready to seize an advantage, we may extricate ourselves from misfortune.

Reduce the hostile chiefs by inflicting damage on them. Make trouble for them, and keep them constantly engaged. Hold out specious allurements, and make them rush to any given point.

The art of war teaches us to rely not on the likelihood of the enemy's not coming, but on our own readiness to receive him; not on the chance of his not attacking, but rather on the fact that we have made our position unassailable.

There are five dangerous faults which may affect a general:

1. Recklessness, which leads to destruction

2. Cowardice, which leads to capture

3. A hasty temper, which can be provoked by insults

4. A delicacy of honor, which is sensitive to shame

5. Over-solicitude for his men, which exposes him to worry and trouble

These are the five besetting sins of a general, ruinous to the conduct of war. When an army is overthrown and its leader slain, the cause will surely be found among these five dangerous faults. Let them be a subject of meditation.

COMMENTARIES

*Chang
Yu said:*

No town should be attacked which, if taken, cannot be held, or if left alone, will not cause any trouble.

*Ts'ao Kung told
this story from his
own experience:*

When invading the territory of Hsu-chou, I ignored the city of Hua-pi, which lay directly in my path, and pressed on into the heart of the country. This excellent strategy was rewarded by the subsequent capture of no fewer than fourteen important district cities.

49

Hsun Ying also,
when urged to attack
the city of Pi-yang, replied:

"The city is small and well fortified. Even if I succeed in taking it, it will be no great feat of arms; whereas if I fail, I shall make myself a laughingstock."

Marshal
Turenne said:

It is a great mistake to waste men in taking a town when the same expenditure of soldiers will gain a province.

Chia Lin told of extenuating
circumstances with reference to the
five obvious and generally
advantageous lines of action:

If a certain road is short, it must be followed. If an army is isolated, it must be attacked. If a town is weak, it must be besieged. If a position can be stormed, it must be attempted. If consistent with military operations, the sovereign's commands must be obeyed. But there are circumstances which sometimes forbid a general to use these advantages. For instance, a certain road may be the shortest way for him, but if he knows that it abounds in natural obstacles, or that the enemy has laid an ambush on it, he will not follow that road. A hostile force may be open to attack, but if he knows that it is hard-pressed and likely to fight with desperation, he will refrain from striking. And so on.

50

*He goes on to
describe several ways
of reducing the hostile chiefs:*

Entice away the enemy's best and wisest men, so that he may be left without counselors. Introduce traitors into his country, that the government policy may be rendered futile. Foment intrigue and deceit, and thus sow dissension between the ruler and his ministers. By means of every artful contrivance, cause deterioration amongst his men and waste of his treasure. Corrupt his morals by insidious gifts leading him into excess. Disturb and unsettle his mind by presenting him with lovely women.

*Of the fault of
over-solicitude,
Lionel Giles said:*

Here Sun Tzu wished to emphasize the danger of sacrificing any important military advantage to the immediate comfort of his men. This is a shortsighted policy, because in the long run the troops will suffer more from the defeat, or, at best, the prolongation of the war, which will be the consequence.

Mountains, rivers, marshes, plains; understanding the enemy; training soldiers.

THE ARMY ON THE MARCH

Sun
Tzu
said:

WE COME NOW TO THE QUESTION of encamping the army, and observing signs of the enemy.

Pass quickly over mountains, and keep in the neighborhood of valleys.

Camp in high places, facing the sun—not on high hills, but on knolls or hillocks elevated above the surrounding country.

Do not climb heights in order to fight.

So much for mountain warfare.

After crossing a river, you should get far away from it.

When an invading force crosses a river in its onward march, do not advance to meet it in midstream. It will be best to let half the army get across, and then deliver your attack.

If you are anxious to fight, you should not go to meet the invader near a river which he has to cross. Moor your craft higher up than the enemy, and facing the sun. Do not move upstream to meet the enemy.

So much for river warfare.

In crossing salt marshes, your sole concern should be to get over them quickly, without any delay. If forced to fight in a salt marsh, you should have water and grass near you, and get your back to a clump of trees.

So much for operations in salt marshes.

In dry, level country, take up an easily accessible position with rising ground to your right and on your rear, so that the danger may be in front, and safety lie behind.

So much for campaigning in flat country.

These—mountains, rivers, marshes, and plains—are the four useful branches of military knowledge which enabled the Yellow Emperor to vanquish four sovereigns.

All armies prefer high ground to low, and sunny places to dark.

If you are careful for your men, and camp on hard ground, the army will be free from disease of every kind, and this will spell victory.

When you come to a hill or a bank, occupy the sunny side, with the slope on your right rear. Thus you will act for the benefit of your soldiers and utilize the natural advantages of the ground.

When, in consequence of heavy rains up-country, a river which you wish to ford is swollen and flecked with foam, you must wait until it subsides.

Country in which there are precipitous cliffs with torrents running between, deep natural hollows, confined places, tangled thickets, quagmires, and crevasses, should be left with all possible speed, or else not approached. While we keep away from such places, we should get the enemy to approach them. While we face such places, we should let the enemy have them on his rear.

If in the neighborhood of your camp there is any hilly country, ponds surrounded by aquatic grass, hollow basins filled with reeds, or woods with thick undergrowth, they must be carefully routed out and searched, for these are places where men in ambush or insidious spies are likely to be lurking.

When the enemy is close at hand and remains quiet, he is relying on the natural strength of his position. When he keeps aloof and tries to provoke a battle, he is anxious for the other side to advance. If his place of encampment is easy of access, he is offering you bait.

Movement among the trees of a forest shows that the enemy is advancing.

The appearance of unlikely objects in the midst of thick grass means that the enemy wants to make us suspicious.

The rising of birds into flight is the sign of an ambush. Startled beasts indicate that a sudden attack is coming.

When there is dust rising in a high column, it is the sign of chariots advancing. When the dust is low, and spread over a wide area, it betokens the approach of infantry. When it branches out in different directions, it shows that parties have been sent to collect firewood. A few clouds of dust moving to and fro signify that the army is encamping.

Humble words and increased preparations are signs that the enemy is about to advance. Violent language and driving forward as if to attack are signs that he will retreat.

When the light chariots come out first and take up a position on the wings, it is a sign that the enemy is forming for battle.

Peace proposals unaccompanied by a sworn covenant indicate a plot.

When there is much running about and the soldiers fall into rank, it means that the critical moment has come.

When some are seen advancing and some retreating, it is a lure.

When the soldiers stand leaning on their spears, they are faint from want of food. If those who are sent to draw water begin by drinking themselves, the army is suffering from thirst. If the enemy sees an advantage to be gained and makes no effort to secure it, the soldiers are exhausted.

If birds gather on any spot, it is unoccupied—a useful way to tell that the enemy has abandoned his camp.

Clamor by night betokens nervousness. If there is disturbance in the camp, the general's authority is weak. If the banners and flags are shifted about, sedition is afoot. If the officers are angry, it means that the men are weary.

When an army feeds its horses with grain and kills its cattle for food, and when the men do not hang their cooking pots over the campfires, showing that they will not return to their tents, you may know that they are determined to fight to the death.

The sight of men whispering together in small knots or speaking in subdued tones points to disaffection among the rank and file.

Too frequent rewards signify that the enemy is at the end of his resources. Too many punishments betray a condition of dire distress.

To begin by bluster, but afterward to take fright at the enemy's numbers, shows a supreme lack of intelligence.

When envoys are sent with compliments in their mouths, it is a sign that the enemy wishes for a truce.

If the enemy's troops march up angrily and remain facing ours for a long time without either joining battle or taking themselves off again, the situation is one that demands great vigilance and circumspection.

If our troops are no more in number than the enemy, that is amply sufficient. It only means that no direct attack can be made. What we can do is simply to concentrate all our available strength, keep a close watch on the enemy, and obtain reinforcements.

He who exercises no forethought but makes light of his opponents is sure to be captured by them.

If soldiers are punished before they have grown attached to you, they will not prove submissive; and, unless submissive, they will be practically useless. If, when the soldiers have become attached to you, punishments are not enforced, the soldiers will still be useless. Therefore soldiers must be treated in the first instance with humanity, but kept under control by means of iron discipline.

This is a certain road to victory.

If, in training soldiers, commands are habitually enforced, the army will be well-disciplined. If not, its discipline will be bad.

If a general shows confidence in his men but always insists on his orders being obeyed, the gain will be mutual.

COMMENTARIES

Tu Mu
said:

Do not linger among barren uplands, but keep close to supplies of water and grass.

Chang Yu supported
this idea with the following story:

Ma Yuan was sent to exterminate the robber captain Wu-tu Ch'iang, who had found a refuge in the hills. Ma Yuan made no attempt to force a battle, but seized all the favorable positions commanding supplies of water and forage. Ch'iang was soon in such a desperate plight for want of provisions that he was forced to make a total surrender. He did not know the advantage of keeping in the neighborhood of valleys.

57

*Li Ch'uan told of
the great victory won
by Han Hsin over
Lung Chu at the Wei River:*

The two armies were drawn up on opposite sides of the river. In the night, Han Hsin ordered his men to take some ten thousand sacks filled with sand and construct a dam a little higher up. Then, leading half his army across, he attacked Lung Chu. After a time, pretending to have failed in his attempt, he hastily withdrew to the other bank. Lung Chu was much elated by this unlooked-for success, and exclaiming, "I felt sure that Han Hsin was really a coward!" he pursued him and began crossing the river in his turn. Han Hsin now sent a party to cut open the sandbags, thus releasing a great volume of water, which swept down and prevented the greater portion of Lung Chu's army from getting across. He then turned upon the force which had been cut off, and annihilated it, Lung Chu himself being among the slain. The rest of the army, on the further bank, also scattered and fled in all directions.

*Mei
Yao-ch'en
said:*

High ground is not only more agreeable, but more convenient from a military point of view. Low ground is not only damp and unhealthy, but also disadvantageous for fighting.

58

Chang Yu quoted
Wei Liao Tzu:

The art of giving orders is not to try to rectify minor blunders and not to be swayed by petty doubts.

Six kinds
of ground,
balancing
the forces
within the army,
fame.

*t*ERRAIN

*Sun
Tzu
said:*

WE MAY DISTINGUISH SIX KINDS OF TERRAIN: accessible ground, entangling ground, standstill ground, narrow passes, precipitous heights, and positions at a great distance from the enemy.

Ground which can be freely traversed by both sides is called *accessible*. With ground of this nature, be before the enemy in occupying the raised and sunny spots, and carefully guard your line of supplies. Then you will be able to fight with advantage.

Ground which can be abandoned but is hard to reoccupy is called *entangling*. From a position of this sort, if the enemy is unprepared, you may sally forth and defeat him. But if the enemy is prepared for your coming, and you fail to defeat him, then, return being impossible, disaster will ensue.

When the position is such that neither side will gain by making the first move, it is called *standstill ground*. Each side finds it difficult to move, and the situation remains at a deadlock. In a position of this sort, even though the enemy should offer attractive bait, it will be advisable not to stir forth, but rather to retreat, thus enticing the enemy in his turn. Then, when part of his army has come out, we may deliver our attack with advantage.

With regard to *narrow passes*, if you can occupy them first, let them be strongly garrisoned and await the advent of the enemy. Should the enemy forestall you in occupying a pass, do not go after him if the pass is fully garrisoned, but only if it is weakly garrisoned.

With regard to *precipitous heights*, if you arrive before your adversary, occupy the raised and sunny spots, and there wait for him to come up. If the enemy has occupied precipitous heights before you, do not follow him, but retreat and try to entice him away.

If you are situated at a *great distance* from the enemy, and the strength of the two armies is equal, it is not easy to provoke a battle, and fighting will be to your disadvantage.

These six are the principles connected with Earth. The general who has attained a responsible post must be careful to study them.

An army may be exposed to six calamities not arising from natural causes, but from faults for which the general is responsible. These are: flight, insubordination, collapse, ruin, disorganization, and rout.

Other conditions being equal, if one force is hurled against another ten times its size, the result will be the *flight* of the former.

When the common soldiers are too strong and their officers too weak, the result is *insubordination*.

When the officers are too strong and the common soldiers too weak, the result is *collapse*.

When the higher officers are angry and insubordinate, and on meeting the enemy give battle on their own account from a feeling of resentment, before the commander-in-chief can tell whether or not he is in a position to fight, the result is *ruin*.

When the general is weak and without authority, when his orders are not clear and distinct, when there are no fixed duties assigned to officers and men, and the ranks are formed in a slovenly, haphazard manner, the result is utter *disorganization*.

When a general, unable to estimate the enemy's strength, allows an inferior force to engage a larger one, or hurls a weak detachment against a powerful one, and neglects to place picked soldiers in the front rank, the result must be a *rout*.

These are six ways of courting defeat, which must be carefully noted by the general who has attained a responsible post.

The natural formation of the country is the soldier's best ally. But the power of estimating the adversary, of controlling the forces of victory, and of shrewdly calculating difficulties, dangers, and distances constitutes the test of a great general. He who knows these things, and in fighting puts his knowledge into practice, will win his battles. He who knows them not, nor practices them, will surely be defeated.

If fighting is sure to result in victory, then you must fight, even though the ruler forbid it. If fighting will not result in victory, then you must not fight, even at the ruler's bidding.

The general who advances without coveting fame and retreats without fearing disgrace, whose only thought is to protect his country and do good service for his sovereign, is the jewel of the kingdom.

Regard your soldiers as your children, and they will follow you into the deepest valleys. Look on them as your own beloved sons, and they will stand by you even unto death.

If, however, you are indulgent, but unable to make your authority felt; kindhearted, but unable to enforce your commands; and incapable, moreover, of quelling disorder—then your soldiers must be likened to spoiled children. They are useless for any practical purpose.

If we know that our own men are in a condition to attack, but are unaware that the enemy is not open to attack, we have gone only halfway toward victory. If we know that the enemy is open to attack, but are unaware that our own men are not in a condition to attack, we have gone only halfway toward victory. If we know that the enemy is open to attack, and also know that our men are in a condition to attack, but are unaware that the nature of the ground makes fighting impracticable, we have still gone only halfway toward victory.

The experienced soldier, once in motion, is never bewildered. Once he has broken camp, he is never at a loss. Hence the saying: If you know the enemy and know yourself, your victory will not stand in doubt. If you know Heaven and know Earth, you may make your victory complete.

COMMENTARIES

Chang Yu told this story
about P'ei Hsing-chien,
who was sent on a punitive
expedition against the Turkic tribes:

At nightfall he pitched his camp as usual, and it had already been completely fortified by wall and ditch when suddenly he gave orders that the army should shift its quarters to a hill nearby. This was highly displeasing to his officers, who protested loudly against the extra fatigue which it would entail on the men. P'ei Hsing-chien, however, paid no heed to their remonstrances and had the camp moved as quickly as possible. Later that night a terrific storm came on, which flooded their former place of encampment to the depth of over twelve feet. The recalcitrant officers were amazed at the sight, and owned that they had been in the wrong. "How did you know what was going to happen?" they asked. P'ei Hsing-chien replied: "From this time forward be content to obey orders without asking unnecessary questions."

*Ch'en Hao defined the six
ways of courting defeat as follows:*

Neglect to estimate the enemy's strength; want of authority; defective training; unjustifiable anger; non-observance of discipline; failure to use picked men.

*Tu Mu told this story of the
famous general Wu Ch'i:*

He wore the same clothes and ate the same food as the meanest of his soldiers, refused to have either a horse to ride or a mat to sleep on, carried his own surplus rations wrapped in a parcel, and shared every hardship with his men. One of his soldiers was suffering from an abscess, and Wu Ch'i himself sucked out the virus. The soldier's mother, hearing this, began wailing and lamenting. Somebody asked her: "Why are you crying? Your son is only a common soldier, and yet the commander-in-chief himself has sucked the poison from his sore." The woman replied: "Many years ago, Lord Wu performed a similar service for my husband, who never left him afterward, and finally met his death at the hands of the enemy. And now that he has done the same for my son, he too will fall fighting I know not where."

*Li Ch'uan tells similarly of the Viscount of Ch'u,
whose soldiers were suffering severely from the cold:*

He made a round of the whole army, comforting and encouraging the men; and straightway they felt as if they were clothed in garments lined with silk.

Tu Mu told this story of
Lu Meng during the occupation
of the town of Chiang-ling:

He had given orders to his army not to molest the inhabitants nor take anything from them by force. Nevertheless, a certain officer serving under his banner, who happened to be from the same town as the general, ventured to appropriate a bamboo hat belonging to one of the people in order to wear it over his regulation helmet as a protection against the rain. Lu Meng considered that the fact of his being a native of the same town as the culprit should not be allowed to palliate a clear breach of discipline, and accordingly he ordered his summary execution, the tears rolling down his face, however, as he did so. This act of severity filled the army with wholesome awe, and from that time forth even articles dropped in the highway were not picked up.

tHE NINE
SITUATIONS

*Sun
Tzu
said:*

THE ART OF WAR RECOGNIZES NINE VARIETIES of ground: dispersive ground, facile ground, contentious ground, open ground, ground of intersecting highways, serious ground, difficult ground, hemmed-in ground, desperate ground.

When a chieftain is fighting in his own territory, it is *dispersive ground,* so called because the soldiers, being near to their homes and anxious to see their wives and children, are likely to seize the opportunity afforded by a battle and scatter in every direction.

When he has penetrated into hostile territory, but to no great distance, it is *facile ground*.

Ground that can be of great advantage to either side is *contentious ground*.

Ground on which each side has liberty of movement is *open ground*.

Ground which forms the key to three contiguous states, so that he who occupies it first has most of the empire at his command, is ground of *intersecting highways*.

When an army has penetrated into the heart of hostile country, leaving a number of fortified cities in its rear, it is *serious ground*.

Mountain forests, rugged steeps, marshes and fens— all country that is hard to traverse—this is *difficult ground*.

Ground which is reached through narrow gorges, and from which we can only retire by tortuous paths, so that a small number of the enemy would suffice to crush a large body of our men: this is *hemmed-in ground*.

Ground on which we can only be saved from destruction by fighting without delay: this is *desperate ground*.

On dispersive ground, therefore, fight not. On facile ground, halt not. On contentious ground, attack not. On open ground, do not try to block the enemy's way. On ground of intersecting highways, join hands with your allies. On serious ground, gather in provisions from all sides. In difficult ground, keep steadily on the march. On hemmed-in ground, resort to stratagem. On desperate ground, fight.

68

Those who were called skillful leaders of old knew how to drive a wedge between the enemy's front and rear;

to prevent cooperation between his large and small divisions; to hinder the good troops from rescuing the bad, the officers from rallying their men. When the enemy's men were scattered, they prevented them from gathering. Even when their forces were united, they managed to keep them in disorder. When it was to their advantage, they made a forward move. When otherwise, they stopped still.

If asked how to cope with a great host of the enemy in orderly array and on the point of marching to the attack, I should say: Begin by seizing something that your opponent holds dear; then he will be amenable to your will.

Speed is the essence of war. Take advantage of the enemy's unreadiness, make your way by unexpected routes, and attack unguarded spots.

The following are the principles to be observed by an invading force.

The further you penetrate into a country, the greater will be the solidarity of your troops, and thus the defenders will not prevail against you.

Make forays in fertile country in order to supply your army with food.

Carefully study the well-being of your men, and do not overtax them. Concentrate your energy and hoard your strength.

Keep your army continually on the move, and devise unfathomable plans.

Throw your soldiers into positions whence there is no escape, and they will prefer death to flight. If they will face death, there is nothing they may not achieve. Officers and men alike will put forth their uttermost strength.

Soldiers in desperate straits lose the sense of fear. If there is no place of refuge, they will stand firm. If they are in the heart of a hostile country, they will show a stubborn front. If there is no help for it, they will fight hard. Thus, without waiting to be marshaled, the soldiers will be constantly on the alert. Without waiting to be asked, they will do your will. Without restrictions, they will be faithful. Even without orders, they can be trusted.

Prohibit the studying of omens, and do away with superstitious doubts. Then, until death itself comes, no calamity need be feared.

If our soldiers are not overburdened with money, it is not because they have a distaste for riches. If their lives are not unduly long, it is not because they are disinclined to longevity. The general must see to it that temptations to shirk fighting and grow rich are not thrown in the way of his men.

On the day they are ordered out to battle, your soldiers may weep—those sitting up bedewing their garments, and those lying down letting the tears run down their cheeks. But let them once be brought to bay, and they will display the courage of a Chuan Chu or a Ts'ao Kuei.

The skillful tactician may be likened to the *shuai-jan*. Now the *shuai-jan* is a snake that is found in the Ch'ang mountains. Strike at its head, and you will be attacked by its tail. Strike at its tail, and you will be attacked by its head. Strike at its middle, and you will be attacked by head and tail both.

Asked if an army can be made to imitate the *shuai-jan*, I should answer, Yes. For the men of Wu and the men of Yueh are enemies. Yet if they are crossing a river in the same boat and are caught by a storm, they will come to each other's assistance just as the left hand helps the right.

It is not enough to put one's trust in the tethering of horses and the burying of chariot wheels in the ground. It is not enough to render flight impossible by such mechanical means. You will not succeed unless your men have tenacity and unity of purpose, and, above all, a spirit of sympathetic cooperation. This is the lesson which can be learned from the *shuai-jan*.

The principle on which to manage an army is to set up one standard of courage that all must reach.

How to make the best of both strong and weak is a question involving the proper use of ground.

Thus the skillful general conducts his army just as though he were leading a single man by the hand.

It is the business of a general to be quiet and thus ensure secrecy. He must be upright and just, and thus maintain order. He must be able to mystify his officers and men by false reports and appearances, and thus keep them in total ignorance.

By altering his arrangements and changing his plans, the leader keeps the enemy without definite knowledge. By shifting his camp and taking circuitous routes, he prevents the enemy from anticipating his purpose.

At the critical moment, the leader of an army acts like one who has climbed up a height and then kicks away the ladder behind him. He carries his men deep into hostile territory before he shows his hand. He burns his boats and breaks his cooking pots. Like a shepherd driving a flock of sheep, he drives his men this way and that, and none knows whither he is going.

It is the business of the general to muster his host and bring it into danger.

The different measures suited to the nine varieties of ground; the expediency of aggressive or defensive tactics; and the fundamental laws of human nature: these are things that must most certainly be studied.

When invading hostile territory, the general principle is: penetrating deeply brings cohesion; penetrating but a short way means dispersion.

When you leave your own country behind and take your army across neighboring territory, you find yourself on critical ground.

When there are means of communication on all four sides, the ground is one of intersecting highways.

When you penetrate deeply into a country, it is serious ground.

When you penetrate but a little way, it is facile ground.

When you have the enemy's strongholds on your rear, and narrow passes in front, it is hemmed-in ground.

When there is no place of refuge at all, it is desperate ground.

Therefore, on dispersive ground, I would inspire my men with unity of purpose.

On facile ground, I would see that there is close connection between all parts of my army.

On contentious ground, I would hurry up my rear guard.

On open ground, I would keep a vigilant eye on my defenses.

On ground of intersecting highways, I would consolidate my alliances.

On serious ground, I would try to ensure a continuous stream of supplies.

On difficult ground, I would keep pushing on along the road.

On hemmed-in ground, I would block any way of retreat.

On desperate ground, I would proclaim to my soldiers the hopelessness of saving their lives.

For it is the soldier's disposition to offer an obstinate resistance when surrounded, to fight hard when he cannot help himself, and to obey promptly when he has fallen into danger.

We cannot enter into alliance with neighboring princes until we are acquainted with their designs. We are not fit to lead an army on the march unless we are familiar with the face of the country—its mountains and forests, its pitfalls and precipices, its marshes and swamps. We shall be unable to turn natural advantages to account unless we make use of local guides.

73

To be ignorant of any one of the following principles does not befit a warlike prince.

When a warlike prince attacks a powerful state, his generalship shows itself in preventing the concentration of the enemy's forces. He overawes his opponents, and their allies are prevented from joining against him.

Hence he does not strive to ally himself with all and sundry, nor does he foster the power of other states. He carries out his own secret designs, keeping his antagonists in awe. Thus he is able to capture their cities and overthrow their kingdoms.

Bestow rewards without regard to rule, issue orders without regard to previous arrangements, and you will be able to handle a whole army as though you had to do with but a single man.

Confront your soldiers with the deed itself. Never let them know your design. When the outlook is bright, bring it before their eyes; but tell them nothing when the situation is gloomy.

Place your army in deadly peril, and it will survive. Plunge it into desperate straits, and it will come through in safety. For it is precisely when a force has fallen into harm's way that it is capable of striking a blow for victory.

Success in warfare is gained by carefully accommodating ourselves to the enemy's purpose.

By persistently hanging on the enemy's flank, we shall succeed in the long run in killing the commander-in-chief.

74

This is called the ability to accomplish a thing by sheer cunning.

On the day that you take up your command, block the frontier passes, destroy all passports and permits, and stop the passage of all emissaries either to or from the enemy's country.

Be stern in the council chamber, so that you may control the situation.

If the enemy leaves a door open, you must rush in.

Forestall your opponent by seizing what he holds dear, and subtly contrive to time his arrival on the ground.

Walk in the path defined by rule, and accommodate yourself to the enemy until you can fight a decisive battle.

At first, exhibit the coyness of a maiden, so that the enemy will open his door. Afterward, move with the speed of a hare, and it will be too late for the enemy to oppose you.

COMMENTARIES

Ch'en Hao
said:

To be on desperate ground is like sitting in a leaking boat or crouching in a burning house.

Ho Shih told the
following anecdote
about speed:

Li Ching was sent to reduce the rebel Hsiao Hsien, who had set up as Emperor at Ching-chou Fu. It was autumn, and the Yangtsze being then in flood, Hsiao Hsien never dreamed that his adversary would venture to come down through the gorges, and consequently made no preparations. But Li Ching embarked his army without loss of

75

time, and was just about to start when the other generals implored him to postpone his departure until the river was in a less dangerous state for navigation. Li Ching replied: "To the soldier, overwhelming speed is of paramount importance, and he must never miss opportunities. Now is the time to strike, before Hsiao Hsien even knows that we have got an army together. If we seize the present moment when the river is in flood, we shall appear before his capital with startling suddenness, like the thunder which is heard before you have the time to stop your ears against it. This is the great principle in war. Even if he gets to know of our approach, he will have to levy his soldiers in such a hurry that they will not be fit to oppose us. Thus the full fruits of victory will be ours." All came about as he predicted, and Hsiao Hsien was obliged to surrender, nobly stipulating that his people should be spared and he alone suffer the penalty of death.

Ch'en told this story of General Wang Chien,
who had invaded the Ch'u State, where a
universal draft was instituted to oppose him:

Being doubtful of the temper of his troops, Wang Chien declined all invitations to fight, and remained strictly on the defensive. In vain did the Ch'u general try to force a battle. Day after day Wang Chien kept inside his walls and would not come out, but devoted his whole time and energy to winning the affection and confidence of his men. He took care that they should be well fed, sharing his own meals with them, provided facilities for bathing, and employed every method of judicious indulgence to weld them into a loyal and homogeneous body. After some time had elapsed,

76

he told certain persons to find out how the men were amusing themselves. The answer was that they were competing with one another at lifting weights and broad jumps. When Wang Chien heard that they were engaged in these athletic pursuits, he knew that their spirits had been strung up to the required pitch and that they were now ready for fighting. By this time the Ch'u army, after repeating their challenge again and again, had marched away eastward in disgust. Wang Chien immediately broke up his camp and followed them, and in the battle that ensued they were routed with great slaughter.

Ts'ao Kung said
this of soldiers
weeping:

This is not because they are afraid, but because all have embraced the firm resolution to do or die.

Chuan Chu and Ts'ao Kuei were heroes known for personal valor. Chuan Chu committed an assassination at the cost of his life, while Ts'ao Kuei, during a delicate treaty negotiation, held a knife against the chest of his opponent until he was promised full restitution of lands.

Tu Yu
said:

77

Burn your baggage, throw away your supplies, choke up the wells, destroy your cooking stoves, and make it plain to your men that they cannot survive, but must fight to the death.

*Mei Yao-ch'en
said:*

The only chance of life lies in giving up all hope of it.

*Chang Yu, speaking
of being deeply
involved in a perilous
position, told this story:*

When Pan Ch'ao arrived at Shan-shan, Kuang, the king of the country, received him with great politeness and respect. But shortly afterward his behavior underwent a sudden change, and he became remiss and negligent. Pan Ch'ao spoke about this to his officers: "Have you not noticed," he said, "that Kuang's polite attentions are on the wane? This must signify that envoys have come from the Northern barbarians, and that consequently he is in a state of indecision, not knowing with which side to throw in his lot." Thereupon he called one of the natives who had been assigned to his service, and set a trap for him, saying: "Where are those envoys from the Hsiung-nu who arrived some days ago?" The man was so taken aback that between surprise and fear he presently blurted out the whole truth. Pan Ch'ao, keeping his informant carefully under lock and key, then summoned a gathering of his officers, thirty-six in all, and began drinking with them. When the wine had mounted into their heads a little, he tried to rouse their spirit still further by addressing them thus: "Gentlemen, here we are in the heart of an isolated region, anxious to achieve riches and honor by some great exploit. Now it happens that an ambassador from the

78

Hsiung-nu arrived in this kingdom only a few days ago, and the result is that the respectful courtesy extended toward us by our royal host has disappeared. Should this envoy prevail upon him to seize our party and hand us over to the Hsiung-nu, our bones will become food for the wolves of the desert. What are we to do?" With one accord, the officers replied, "Standing as we do in peril of our lives, we will follow our commander through life and death."

Mei Yao-ch'en constructed
this chain of reasoning:

In attacking a powerful state, if you can divide her forces, you will have a superiority in strength. If you have a superiority in strength, you will overawe the enemy. If you overawe the enemy, the neighboring states will be frightened. If the neighboring states are frightened, the enemy's allies will be prevented from joining her.

Chang Yu and
Chin Lin said:

Your arrangements should not be divulged beforehand. There should be no fixity in your rules and arrangements.

79

Cultivating

resources.

ATTACK BY FIRE AND WATER

Sun
Tzu
said:

THERE ARE FIVE WAYS OF ATTACKING WITH FIRE. The first is to burn soldiers in their camp. The second is to burn supplies. The third is to burn baggage trains. The fourth is to burn arsenals and magazines. The fifth is to hurl dropping fire among the enemy.

In order to carry out an attack with fire, we must have means available. The material for raising fire should always be kept in readiness.

There is a proper season for making attacks with fire, and special days for starting a conflagration. The proper season is when the weather is very dry. The special days are those when the moon is in the constellations of the Sieve, the Wall, the Wing, or the Crossbar, for these four are all days of rising wind.

In attacking with fire, one should be prepared to meet five possible developments.

1. When fire breaks out inside the enemy's camp, respond at once with an attack from without.

2. If there is an outbreak of fire, but the enemy's soldiers remain quiet, bide your time and do not attack.

3. When the force of the flames has reached its height, follow it up with an attack, if that is practicable. If not, stay where you are.

4. If it is possible to make an assault with fire from without, do not wait for it to break out within, but deliver your attack at a favorable moment.

5. When you start a fire, be to the windward of it. Do not attack from the leeward.

A wind that rises in the daytime lasts long, but a night breeze soon falls.

In every army, the five developments connected with fire must be known, the movements of the stars calculated, and a watch kept for the proper days.

Hence those who use fire as an aid to the attack show intelligence.

Those who use water as an aid to the attack gain an accession of strength. By means of water, an enemy may be intercepted, but not robbed of all his belongings.

Unhappy is the fate of one who tries to win his battles and succeed in his attacks without cultivating the spirit of enterprise, for the result is waste of time and general stagnation.

Hence the saying: The enlightened ruler lays his plans well ahead; the good general cultivates his resources.

Move not unless you see an advantage. Use not your troops unless there is something to be gained. Fight not unless the position is critical.

No ruler should put troops into the field merely to satisfy his own rage. No general should fight a battle simply out of anger. Anger may in time change to gladness. Vexation may be succeeded by content. But a kingdom that has once been destroyed can never come again into being, nor can the dead ever be brought back to life.

Hence, the enlightened ruler is heedful, and the good general full of caution. This is the way to keep a country at peace and an army intact.

COMMENTARIES

*Tu Mu illustrated
the principles of attack
by fire with these anecdotes:*

82

The famous Li Ling once baffled the leader of the Hsiung-nu when the latter, taking advantage of a favorable wind, tried to set fire to the Chinese general's camp only to find that every scrap of combustible vegetation in the neighborhood had already been burned down.

On the other hand, Po-ts'ai, a general of the Yellow Turban rebels, was badly defeated through his neglect of this simple precaution. At the head of a large army, he was besieging a very small garrison held by Huang-fu Sung, who called his officers together and said, "In war, there are various indirect methods of attack, and numbers do not count for everything. Now the rebels have pitched their camp in the midst of thick grass which will easily burn when the wind blows. If we set fire to it at night they will be thrown into a panic, and we can make a sortie and attack them on all sides at once." That evening a strong breeze sprang up. So Huang-fu Sung instructed his soldiers to bind reeds together into torches and mount guard on the city walls, after which he sent out a band of daring men who stealthily made their way through the lines and started the fire with loud shouts and yells. Simultaneously, a glare of light shot up from the city walls, and Huang-fu Sung, sounding his drums, led a rapid charge, which threw the rebels into confusion and put them to headlong flight.

Tu Mu
said:

If the wind is in the east, begin burning to the east of the enemy, and follow up the attack yourself from that side. If you start a fire on the east side, and then attack from the west, you will suffer in the same way as your enemy.

*Regarding the
enlightened ruler,
Tu Mu said:*

The warlike prince controls his soldiers by his authority, knits them together by good faith, and keeps them loyal by means of rewards. If faith decays, there will be disruption. If rewards are deficient, commands will not be respected.

Divine

manipulation

of the

threads.

THE USE
OF SPIES

RAISING A HOST OF A HUNDRED THOUSAND MEN and marching them great distances entails heavy loss on the people and a drain on the resources of the state. The daily expenditure will amount to a thousand ounces of silver. There will be commotion at home and abroad, and men will drop down exhausted on the highways. As many as seven hundred thousand families will be impeded in their labor.

Hostile armies may face each other for years, striving for the victory that is decided in a single day. This being so, to remain in ignorance of the enemy's condition, simply because one grudges the outlay of a hundred ounces of silver in honors and fees, is the height of inhumanity.

One who acts thus is no leader of men, no help to his sovereign, and no master of victory.

What enables the wise sovereign and the good general to strike and conquer, achieving things beyond the reach of ordinary men, is *foreknowledge.*

Now this foreknowledge cannot be elicited from spirits. It cannot be obtained inductively from experience, nor by any deductive calculation.

Knowledge of the enemy's dispositions can only be obtained from other men.

Hence the use of spies, of whom there are five classes: local spies, internal spies, converted spies, doomed spies, surviving spies.

When these five kinds of spies are all at work, none can discover the secret system.

This is called "divine manipulation of the threads."

It is the sovereign's most precious faculty.

Having *local spies* means employing the services of the inhabitants of a district.

Having *internal spies* means making use of officials of the enemy.

Having *converted spies* means getting hold of the enemy's spies and using them for our own purposes.

Having *doomed spies* means doing certain things openly for purposes of deception, and allowing our own spies to know of them and report them to the enemy.

Surviving spies, finally, are those who bring back news from the enemy's camp.

Hence it follows there must be no more intimate relations in the whole army than those maintained with spies. No one should be more liberally rewarded. And nowhere else should greater secrecy be preserved.

Spies cannot be usefully employed without a certain intuitive sagacity.

Spies cannot be properly managed without benevolence and directness.

Without subtle ingenuity of mind, one cannot make certain of the truth of their reports.

Be subtle! Be subtle! And use your spies for every kind of business.

If a secret piece of news is divulged by a spy before the time is ripe, he must be put to death together with the person to whom the secret was told.

Whether the object be to crush an army, to storm a city, or to assassinate an individual, it is always necessary to begin by finding out the names of the attendants, the aides-de-camp, the doorkeepers and sentries of the general in command. Our spies must be commissioned to ascertain these.

The enemy's spies who have come to spy on us must be sought out, tempted with bribes, led away and comfortably housed. Thus they will become converted spies and available for our service.

It is through the information brought by the converted spy that we are able to acquire and employ local and internal spies. It is owing to his information, again, that we can cause the doomed spy to carry false tidings to the enemy. Lastly, it is by his information that the surviving spy can be used on appointed occasions.

The end and aim of spying in all its five varieties is knowledge of the enemy. And this knowledge can only be derived, in the first instance, from the converted spy. Hence it is essential that the converted spy be treated with the utmost liberality.

Of old, the rise of the Yin dynasty was due to I Chih, who had served under the Hsia. Likewise, the rise of the Chou dynasty was due to Lu Ya, who had served under the Yin.

Hence it is only the enlightened ruler and the wise general who will use the highest intelligence of the army for purposes of spying, and thereby they achieve great results.

Spies are a most important element in war, because upon them depends an army's ability to move.

COMMENTARIES

*Mei Yao-ch'en
said:*

Knowledge of the spirit world is to be obtained by divination. Information in natural science may be sought by inductive reasoning. The laws of the universe can be verified by mathematical calculation. But the dispositions of the enemy are ascertainable through spies and spies alone.

Tu Mu
said:

In the enemy's country, win people over by kind treatment and use them as spies.

Enumerating those likely to
serve as internal spies, he cited:

Worthy men who have been degraded from office. Criminals who have undergone punishment. Favorite concubines who are greedy for gold. Men who are aggrieved at being in subordinate positions, or who have been passed over in the distribution of posts. Others who are anxious that their side should be defeated in order that they may have a chance of displaying their ability and talents, fickle turncoats who always want to have a foot in each boat. Officials of these kinds should be secretly approached and bound to one's interests by means of rich presents. In this way you will be able to find out the state of affairs in the enemy's country, ascertain the plans that are being formed against you, and, moreover, disturb the harmony and create a breach between the sovereign and his ministers. But there is a necessity for extreme caution in dealing with internal spies.

Of converted spies,
Chang Yu said:

We must tempt the converted spy into our service, because it is he who knows which of the local inhabitants are greedy of gain, and which of the officials are open to corruption.

Of converted spies,
Tu Yu said:

By means of heavy bribes and liberal promises, detach them from the enemy's service and induce them to carry back false information as well as to spy in turn on their own countrymen.

And of
doomed spies:

We do things calculated to deceive our own spies, who must be led to believe that they have been unwittingly disclosed. Then, when these spies are captured in the enemy's lines, they will make an entirely false report, and the enemy will take measures accordingly, only to find that we do something quite different. The spies will thereupon be put to death.

Tu Mu further
spoke of surviving spies:

This is the ordinary class of spies, who should form a regular part of the army. Your surviving spy must be a man of keen intellect, though in outward appearance a fool. He must be of shabby exterior, but with a will of iron. He must be active, robust, and endowed with physical strength and courage. He must be thoroughly accustomed to all sorts of dirty work, able to endure hunger and cold, shame and ignominy.

Of the sagacity required
by one who uses spies,
Tu Mu said:

Before using spies we must assure ourselves as to their integrity of character and the extent of their experience and skill. A brazen face and a crafty disposition are more dangerous than mountains or rivers. It takes a man of genius to penetrate such.

Chia Lin
said:

An army without spies is like a man without ears or eyes.

FIGHTING SOUTH OF THE CASTLE

An anonymous Chinese poem, circa 124 B.C.E.

They fought south of the Castle,
They died north of the wall.
They died in the moors and were not buried.
Their flesh was the food of crows.
"Tell the crows we are not afraid;
We have died in the moors and cannot be buried.
Crows, how can our bodies escape you?"
The waters flowed deep,
And the rushes in the pool were dark.
The riders fought and were slain:
Their horses wander neighing.
By the bridge there was a house.
Was it south, was it north?
The harvest was never gathered.
How can we give you your offerings?
You served your Prince faithfully,
Though all in vain.
I think of you, faithful soldiers;
Your service shall not be forgotten.
For in the morning you went out to battle,
And at night you did not return.